I Am Magic

I Am Magic

KARISHMA KOTHARI

NU VOICE
PRESS

First published by NU VOICE PRESS 2024
An imprint of Hubhawks Pvt. Ltd
www.nuvoicepress.com

This is a work of fiction. Space and time have been rearranged to suit the convenience of the book. Except for public figures, hotels, and institution names, any resemblance to persons living or dead or the real events are purely coincidental. The opinions expressed in the book are those of the characters, and should not be confused with that of the Author.

ISBN: 978-81-980376-7-1

Typeset by Saanvi Graphics, Noida
Printed at Nutech Print Services - India
Published by Nu Voice Press

I dedicate this book to my parents whose love, support and unwavering trust in me made this possible.

Contents

Home

FIGURING OUT LIFE IN A NEW COUNTRY

She is a 'moved-abroad' girl,
Figuring out life in a new world.
Fragile she is, but not weak,
For she stood strong even where there was no one to speak!

Once a pampered, spoilt brat,
Became an independent, strong girl just like that.
The new country taught her at every step,
No matter how hard it was, she had to accept!

Joy she found in getting lost,
While leaving her footprints on the unknown paths she crossed.
The little girl in her was finally screaming,
For the life she had was the one she was dreaming!

From sitting alone in her room to cry,
To dancing and singing under the open sky.
She has done it all,
No matter how many times life made her fall!

MISSING HOME A LITTLE TOO MUCH TODAY

Sitting in the noiseless library, my heart whispered:
I am missing my home.

With a feeling so intense it shatters my heart into a
million pieces,
I dream about the day when I'll be home.

Eyes yearning for the sight of my nearest and dearest,
Heart craving for the laughter, moments, and memories,
And taste buds longing for home-cooked meals.

A place filled with the warmth of childhood,
Beholding so much love and innocence.
A desire surges to feel it all from the beginning,
But I know nothing will be the same again.

Now my heart is full,
Eyes brim with tears, and cheeks are wet,
All I want to do is go home!

DIWALI IS NOT THE SAME ANYMORE

This year, too, Diwali is not the same,
For I won't be in the Diwali family picture frame.
Everyone will be home for the festival of light,
But 7,544 kilometres away, my Diwali is just like a regular night.

I miss the flowers on the street, spreading their aromatic scent,
Every home filled with *rangoli*, *diyas*, and presents.
There is something special about the Diwali air,
Which fills every corner with happiness and prayer!

The festival of lights,
Has lightened up my pink city's dark nights.
How did I gather the strength,
To stay away from home on Diwali for three years at length?

Away from home, it's a never-ending struggle,
Of how to make my Diwali special.
It's just not the same feeling,
And Diwali here no longer has the good, old childhood meaning.

A TRIBUTE TO MY HOMES: INDIA AND THE UK

Sitting on the flight, flying back home,
I realise how fast time has flown.

There is an excitement to go home,
Yet, a strange ache engulfs my heart,
For I have created a new life of my own here.

This country made me independent and responsible,
Taught me that everything is possible,
Guided me to learn from every situation,
By keen observation.

But my country watched me grow as a child,
Seeing me return, it smiled.
I said, "I won't be here for too long."
"Don't worry, I've made you very strong",
My country replied.

Respect and love for both countries I bear in my soul,
For the UK taught me my life's role,
And India gave me the strength to achieve my goal.

Yet, India will always be my sweetheart,
For when I fly to the UK, there's a thrill wrapped in a strange fear,
But when I fly to India, there's only peace with no tears.

"Welcome to the Indira Gandhi International Airport of Delhi",
This line gives me butterflies in my belly.
This moment is the greatest form of satisfaction,
Mere words can't do justice to my reaction!

All I can say is "Thank You" to them,
I shall be indebted to both for making me who I am today!

TO MY LITTLE GIRL, WITH LOVE

Come back, my grown-up girl,
Your home misses that little school girl.
My walls are craving to hear your laughter,
My kitchen is waiting for another baking disaster,
My floor is yearning to feel your not-so-tiny feet,
And your bed is waiting for you to mess up the sheets.

When did you grow up so fast,
And leave me only with the memories of your past?
The girl who came back to me no matter what,
Has suddenly learnt to live without me.

You tell me that you miss me,
That you become homesick too,
But oh, my little girl,
I miss you more than you do.

Don't forget me in this race of life,
And keep coming back to me.
I will gladly take you in with open arms,
And make you feel at home all over again.
For I am just 'home' without you,
It is you, my little girl, who makes me 'home sweet home.'

—Home Sweet Home

SHELTER VERSUS HOME

You will find shelter in many,
But Home—you will find only in one.

—Shelter is temporary, Home is permanent.

Coming of Age

BLANK FACES, BORING LECTURES

Sitting in the classroom all blank,
All I want to be is frank.

Yes, I am not enjoying today's lecture,
Pretending to listen while staring at the screen of the projector.

"How boring can it be?" I think,
While my mind wanders to different places,
And all I can imagine are boys with cute faces.

Looking at the old clock's tick-tock,
And wondering why the time is so slow to walk.

How monotonous can it be?
For the professor knows that everyone is yawning,
Looking for a life with a new dawning.

When asked, "Does the lecture make sense?"
Everyone nods with pretence.

Sitting in the classroom all blank,
All I want to be is frank.

WE GREW UP TOO FAST...

From exchanging notes in school,
To exchanging ideas,
We grew up.

From chasing the school bus,
To chasing goals,
We grew up.

From eating each other's tiffin,
To skipping meals,
We grew up.

From celebrating birthday parties,
To celebrating each other's achievements,
We grew up.

From seeing each other every day in school,
To planning to meet once in a while,
We grew up.

From bunking classes together,
To going to work every day,
We grew up.

From making excuses to not go to school,
To getting emotional on our farewell,
We grew up.

From asking for money from parents,
To making our own money,
We grew up.

From night parties,
To morning gym and jog,
We grew up.

BECAUSE I WILL NEVER BE TWENTY-ONE AGAIN

Because I will never be twenty-one again,
Travelling and exploring unknown cities by myself,
Without a worry of what lies ahead,
With an urge to live a life better in reality than in my head.

Because I will never be twenty-one again,
Fearlessly taking the steps alone,
For I am bored of the known,
And there lies a unique magnetism towards the unknown.

Because I will never be twenty-one again,
As free as a bird flying in the open sky,
Not giving up at my lows and cheering up at my highs,
For I am not answerable to anyone's 'why?'.

Because I will never be twenty-one again,
Crying and laughing at the same time,
For life ahead might be a difficult climb,
But sure I am to make everything rhyme!

Because I will never be twenty-one again,
Saying yes to every adventure and taking risks,
For there must be no regrets at all,
The money spent will be forgotten, big or small,
So, I live a life worth a recall!

WALKING THE UNTRODDEN PATHS OF LIFE

Yes, I am figuring it out,
Keeping plans to myself and avoiding the shout,
For there is mystery in how things will unfold,
And between all the uncertainties, faith is what I tend to hold.

No one has it all figured out,
For the path towards success comes with many changes of routes.
So, take one day at a time,
And do not rush your steps to climb.

Remember, life can never be about prediction,
For there exist miracles, destiny, karma, and God which hold the power to change your destination,
And this makes life about figuring it out.
So, believe in the charm of the unknown,
And embrace the solace of being alone!

DEAR YOUNGER SELF

Dear younger self,

You did it!
You did not give up even after a hit,
You survived all the downs and lows,
You opened the doors that were closed.

You have carved a strong and independent personality,
You have instilled in me a very strong faith for certainty,
You have shown me the way,
Now it's my turn to pay.

I will work hard to fulfil every desire,
For you have ignited within me a fire.
I won't let your expectations go in vain,
I will achieve all your childhood dreams without complaint!

To end with a piece of advice,
A little less stress and overthinking would have been nice,
You were too young to carry that burden,
In the end, nobody cares and all mistakes are forgotten.
Life turned out pretty well, younger me,
Every new phase that unfolded were truly setting me free!

DEAR FUTURE SELF

Dear future self,

You must be sitting on your big leather chair,
With the windows open, allowing the breeze to play with your hair,
Sipping coffee with a novel in your hand,
Thinking how everything turned out perfect and grand.

I'm sure you've made the ten-year-old Karishma proud;
You must've achieved what the twenty-year-old Karishma dreamed of.
And now you must be breathing the air of satisfaction,
With nothing bothering you as a distraction.

I wonder if you still get anxious often, and overthink,
Like the sixteen-year-old Karishma whose moods changed in a blink?
Or has time calmed you down and curtailed your stress and worry?
Time must've taught you many things along life's long journey.

I hope you are still a kid at heart,
Always rejoicing in the little things that form life's greater part.
I know you have more to look back at than look forward to,
For you have lived your life just the way you wanted to.

A FAIRY TALE

Once upon a time,
There was a little girl with dreams in her eyes,
And hope in her heart to live her life under foreign skies.
Between the dreaming and the reality,
Her dreams became her reality and her reality became
her dreams.
Unstoppable she was, who packed eighteen years of her life
and flew,
To a different country, all to make her and her father's
dreams come true.
Three years passed by in the blink of an eye,
And then it was time for her to graduate.
She flung the cap high, carried the degree in her hand,
And told her fourteen-year-old self, "We did it and it turned
out better than what we had planned!"
For she never dreamt of a sky full of stars,
But only aspired for the moon.

This was her fairy tale—to fulfil her biggest dream and see
pride in her parents' eyes for their little girl (who was not so
little anymore),
And this was not the end but the beginning of her happily
ever after.

—To many more such fairy tales.

The Power of Words

TO JOHN KEATING

Read when you want to understand,
Write when you want to be understood.

TO WRITE OR NOT TO WRITE?

Writing is not just typing for me.
It is a way to set my mind free,
Free from all the chaos in my heart,
And to unwind and immerse myself deeply into this art.

Writing gives me peace and hope,
Helps me untangle the knots in my life's rope.

Writing helps me say out loud,
What I would've feared to speak in front of a crowd.

Laying my heart bare,
Expressing the feelings that are rare.
Being an introvert,
Writing is my tool to express my hurt.

Overwhelming at times it becomes,
When all the emotions come rushing in at once,
For I live every moment twice:
First in the present,
And then through writing, I find my paradise.

HOW DID I START WRITING?

Writing rarely comes from a comfort zone,
One has to embrace the unknown,
Let the ego depart,
And experience their dark side to create art.

Missing India did something to me that being in India
would've never done!
It helped me appreciate emptiness and solitude,
It helped me love my own company by changing my attitude,
And most of all, it helped me start writing.

That one flight did change a lot around me but especially
within me,
Sure, I felt a certain void inside,
A void which compelled me to write,
To write about the daily battles I fight.
Before I realised, the void was filled with poetry,
Felt so unreal and just like a mystery,
For I had to experience the emptiness to feel fulfilled all
over again!

POETRY: MY FIRST LOVE

One thing I can purely call mine,
Are the words and poems I design,
I have created them, lived them, and stored them in my heart,
My words will live for generations through my art.

Being a good orator seems easy when you're young,
But for me, words do not easily roll out of my tongue,
The way they roll out of my keyboard.
However, I can't write what I see or when I feel bored,
I can only write what I feel.

Started romanticising my life through poems,
Starting celebrating even the smallest moments to
feel wholesome,
Can't ever stop writing,
Even now, my mind is full of words waiting to be articulated
into poems.

A thought struck me late at night,
Human life is finite!
But how blessed I am to have the power of words,
For I will be able to live forever through my poems!

SNEAK PEEK INTO A POET'S MIND

Let me give you a glimpse of a poet's mind,
Where rivulets of thoughts you will find,
Flowing through many obstacles and hurdles,
Sometimes just moving around in circles.

Our mind is a river brimming with words,
But an entire ocean of feelings exists in our hearts waiting to be heard,
How can we relax our minds even for a second?
Because relaxing means inviting destructive floods in our minds.

Just like a river flowing down a mountain,
Our poems pour out from our minds like a fountain.
However, it's not always perfect and poetic,
It takes our entire being immersed deeply in emotions to make the poems aesthetic.

Even after all this, readers read,
Just a minuscule of what's inside a poet's heart and head,
For some feelings are too precious to be given the form of words,
And words might never do justice to the intensity of those feelings.

TRAPPED IN THE JAIL OF MY THOUGHTS

My mind was a prison of countless thoughts,
And I, being both the prison and the prisoner,
Was bound by the cage and had no way to escape.

It was only my pen that had the key to unlock the lock,
And that was it—writing became my passage,
To enter into a world which was purely mine,
Where I could walk, run, jump, fly and be the designer as well as the design.

WRITER'S BLOCK: PARADOX OF THE UNWRITTEN

Clicking my long nails on the cup of green tea,
Tapping my toes one, two, and three,
Staring blankly at my laptop screen,
Disappointed at my inability to create a poetic scene.

Restless is what I am feeling,
For failing to fetch words with meaning.
Typing and pressing backspace,
That's what I am doing with an anxious pace.

Hate to name it,
But it's the writer's block that messes with my wit.
No one can lend me a creative hand to write,
It's me who has to pull myself out from the dark towards
the light.

As I take the last sip of my green tea,
I look up and pray for the creativity key,
To unlock the block,
And start writing without looking at the clock.

OH, TO GO ON LIVING EVEN AFTER DEATH!

I am a poet but someday I wish to become a poem written with black ink in a vintage book pressed between dried roses eternalising myself till the apocalypse.

I want to leave my mark long after I've left.

BECOMING HER OWN MUSE

When the world gave her a bruise,
She had no choice but to become her own muse.
Her search for inspiration ended,
When she no longer hid her true self and pretended.

She found out the real her,
She, who had been through it all,
And despite the hardships, standing strong,
And trusting God all along.

Neither did she find the inspiration,
Nor did she choose writing as her occupation,
For inspiration came and found her,
And labelled her as its favourite to bask in the joy of writing.

She being the child of creativity,
Loved to talk daily to the divinity.
For the higher powers had her back,
Which saved her and her art from every attack.

A simple prayer she chanted,
"Dear God of writing, the one who grants
Children the ability to turn words into art,
Please bestow upon me the power,
To put words to the feelings in my heart!"

WORDS: A WRITER'S WEAPON

Not all writers write from sorrow,
Some use their life's experiences as their arrow,
To strike with words which pierce right through the heart,
And show the reader the world from their eyes through
their art.

How magnificent it is to have such a power,
To play with words at every hour,
For we can immortalise our love,
By capturing them in our words!

It takes a little less than being complete,
To be able to articulate feelings into words on repeat.
Writing helps them release,
That which took away their peace.

Writers know the struggle,
When everything in their mind is juggled.
For even with words as our weapon,
It is very tough to pen down some confessions.

MY ETERNAL LOVE FOR BOOKS

Immerse me in the world of books,
For I truly belong
Between the pages of a book,
Trying to find myself between right and wrong.

The freshness of new books brings out,
The excitement of new beginnings without a doubt.
And at the same time, the evocative smell of worn-out books,
Plays as a reminder of a past that was overcome by hook or by
crook.

Books carry within them a special power,
Power to transport us to a place that planes can never at
any hour,
Power to see ourselves from a different frame of mind,
And power to see things to which our eyes are blind.

Books often make me wonder,
"Who was I?", "Who am I?", and "Who might I become?"
Maybe I am a blend of all the books I read,
Waiting to be written and read.

A POET'S SECRET

I can immortalize,
Or destroy you with my words.
There is nothing in between,
For it is always either of the two extremes!

—Power of a writer or poet using words as their weapon.

My Mind and Me

SHE IS THE PHOENIX

There's fire in her eyes,
From the ashes she will rise.
She is the phoenix bird,
Her glory will be seen and heard.

Her eyes have seen hell,
From being submissive, she has become a rebel.
She has understood her worth,
Now it is time to see the change and witness her rebirth.

With victory reflecting in her eyes,
Conquering her conquests with no cries,
No longer a victim to all the misery,
She has begun her ride towards victory.

THE PARADOX OF LONELINESS

Am I getting used to the loneliness around me?
It scares and amazes me at the same time,
For I am amazed at doing everything alone,
And scared too, for I crave the presence of someone known.

The darkness looms over me,
As it gets quieter and colder.
Seems like the empty room mocks,
For it has been a while since the door heard any knocks.

It's just my heartbeat that I hear,
And every beat misses the ones who are not near.
It's just me and my silence,
Sitting together and missing my loved ones' presence.

The nights and pillows know my secret,
How every night I want to quit
And run back home,
But the mirror shows me who I am and how far I've flown.

SOMETIMES I AM MY OWN ENEMY

Can I switch off my mind?
Overthinking is making me blind.
It is consuming and killing me all at once,
For my head is never at rest and always on the run.

Why am I thinking too much?
Maybe because I am feeling too much.
The way I am questioning in my head,
And generating hundreds of answers before going to bed.

Can I numb my emotions?
For I am tired of swimming in the deep oceans!
Feeling every little thing with great intensity,
Makes me wonder why I can't be heartless and free from all perplexity!

My heart refuses to beat,
Without feeling a little too much with every heartbeat!
All the emotions rupture from my heart,
And find their way out through my eyes.

My insecurities strangle my mind every night,
And my inner self struggles and fights,
With every thought crossing my mind,
Begging it to rest and leave the grind.

I AM THERE FOR MYSELF

Being my own cheerleader,
Patting my own shoulder,
I remind myself of all the battles I've fought and won,
And how strong I am to not escape from the run.

Reassuring myself every day,
Trusting God and continuing to pray,
Just a few more steps to take,
Before everything falls into place without a break.

Came too far to give up and leave,
As quitting is for the weak who couldn't believe,
That even after being shattered and crushed,
Life goes on with unwavering trust.

I know I can pull myself out of the mess,
For even after the storms sent to destroy me,
I found myself braving the cold, dark night,
As I've been raised not to give up, but to fight.

DEAR TWENTY-SOMETHING

Dear twenty-something,

I know life is full of question marks right now,
Which direction will my career take and how?
Do I have time, or do I need to start now?
What will my future partner look like?
And so on, there are many things between us alike.

Life might feel like a treadmill,
While constantly running behind your wants and your will.
When nothing seems to work in your favour,
Take a break.
Maybe it's time for you to change your direction,
Remember, it's not too late to set a good impression.

Recall how desperately you wanted to be this age ten years ago,
This age is to trust the process and grow.
After ten years,
Everything will be sorted, including our careers,
And we'll laugh at our unnecessary worries with eyes full of happy tears.

YES, I AM DIFFERENT

Yes, I don't enjoy clubbing,
Some might think of me as an introvert,
But the real truth remains hidden,
Never had the strength to say so now it's being written.

Can't imagine being a part of the crowd,
Don't want to be someone who hoots and shouts out loud.
It feels like a sheer waste of energy,
Just for a few hours' fun, an entire day sacrificed to lethargy.

Tried clubbing maybe once or twice,
Realised soon enough that it comes with a price.
Price in terms of your time,
For time is money and wasting it feels like a crime.

Initially experienced the fear of missing out,
But now deep down, I have the satisfaction of missing out.

Honestly, I don't have time to commit mistakes and learn,
So I learn from others' mistakes and when it feels wrong, I take a U-turn.
I trust that I am different for a special cause,
Maybe God is preparing me for something beyond a pause!

REJECTION: A BLESSING IN DISGUISE

Even after working hard for an eternity,
I was rejected by my dream university.
I grieved my inability to secure a place,
Was left heartbroken and unwilling to accept reality in my face.

Gathered some strength and waited to hear from other colleges,
Yes, other colleges did send their acknowledgements,
But the University that was my dream,
Didn't accept me in their stream.

After going to the university that accepted me,
I realised that the rejection had actually set me free.
I understood my place at my university and felt belonged,
And couldn't have felt this happy at any other place for which I longed.

That single rejection unknowingly strengthened my core,
For I understood the reason behind the rejection.
I was not rejected because I was not ready for them,
I was rejected because they were not ready for me.
Maybe they were threatened by my ability to outshine everyone.

DREAMS, PRAYERS, AND GOD

Day one, day two, day three, day four…
Preparing for the day when I will soar,
Soar high, up in the sky,
Spread my wings and just fly.

Carrying so many dreams in my eyes,
With a small doubt: will I be able to rise?
Read and heard all the motivational speeches,
But nothing seems to mend all the pieces.

Tired from all the overthinking and stress,
Started wondering if Google maps could show me the path towards success,
Until one fine day a realisation came my way,
I finally discovered the Google map I'd been searching every day.

The moment I gave the control of my life to Lord Hanuman,
I magically witnessed a transformation exactly the way I expected,
For I started following the path as he directed.

It feels like I'm not moving, but I steadily move towards my goal,
For he knows the correct rhythm of brake and acceleration
Required for me to head towards my destination.

ALL MY YETS

I am yet to experience some of the greatest treasures of life,
I am yet to live those moments that are yearning to take the shape of a poem,
I am yet to become successful,
I am yet to step foot in countries I've never been to,
I am yet to skydive to view the world from a different perspective,
I am yet to taste all the desserts in the world,
I am yet to read a thousand books,
I am yet to meet the love of my life,
I am yet to have my dream wedding,
I am yet to have kids whom I will nurture all my life.

These 'yets' make me hopeful and excited for the future,
These yet-to-be-fulfilled wishes fill me up with ambition and passion,
For these 'yets' are threads of hope holding me together,
Amidst all the challenges and struggles to achieve them.

If one gets everything one wishes for,
The excitement to live will disappear,
Life will turn mundane,
And nothing will nurture in one's brain,
For some unfulfilled wishes are the reason,
Of dreaming and working towards freedom and a happy season.

THE POWER OF CHOICES

The choices were mine to make,
Having full control over my choice of mistake.
I lost control after the decision,
Now it was my choice's turn to control my life with precision.

One wrong choice,
And I ended up with regret's noise.
The choice that seemed great,
Had suddenly strangled me as its bait.

The consequences that unfolded later,
Turned me into my own traitor,
Despite knowing that I had the control,
I chose something that saddened my soul.

The choice was made, the deal was done,
There was no going back to change that one.
Responsibility for my decisions I hold,
And the only option is to be strong and bold.
For under unfavourable conditions, they carve gold.

HUMBLING DOWN

From reacting to responding,
From being emotional to letting things go,
From being impatient to learning to wait,
Life has humbled me down.

As I am growing up,
I am seeking things which are more down-to-earth.
The feelings of hate and vengeance are diminishing,
And suddenly petty drama is no longer interesting.

Seeing myself choose calm over chaos,
Sneakers over heels,
Home-cooked food over restaurant meals,
A good night's sleep over all-nighters,
I've evolved out of the crazy mess.

Quality is what I have started to crave,
For I realised quantity is for the coward and not the brave.
I finally found the courage to step back,
And not tolerate insults in the form of jokes they crack.

IT WAS HAPPENING AGAIN

Everything was alright,
Until the clock struck midnight.
When everyone was asleep,
My heart started to weep.

It had happened before and it was happening again,
Nights were getting longer,
And my inner storms were getting stronger,
As I found myself stuck between regret and anger.

Weeping, I slept,
And woke up with a pillow that was wet.
Yet again, mornings forced me to put on a smiling face,
So that the world would remain oblivious to my
emotional chase.

Nature

EARTHQUAKE: MOTHER EARTH'S ANGUISHED CRIES

At four in the morning, Mother Earth shook.
She couldn't handle all the pressure it took,
We humans did not treat our Mother Earth well,
And now, her rage was impossible to quell.

Yes, it was an earthquake,
The fast asleep humans were suddenly awake.
Beds and furniture wobbled,
And in a fraction of time, humans were out on the roads, looking troubled.

Felt the quake four times,
Seemed like Mother Earth was screaming to stop our crimes,
Asking her dear children to stop hurting,
In her own unique way of expressing.

The earthquake surely shook the ground beneath our feet,
But it also helped me realised something very concrete.
Imagine all the pain Mother Earth endures,
Just to keep her children safe and secure!

It's not too late to preserve her,
It's not late for our love to be shown.
She has been fighting all the battles alone,
So, let's all protect the land on which we have grown.

THE MOON AND MY SOULMATE

Sitting on the terrace late at night,
Gazing at the moon shining bright,
Feeling the moonlight sparkle in my eyes.
Oh, how beautiful the moon is in every shape and size!

Someone, somewhere might be looking at the same moon,
With glittering eyes full of wonder, just like mine.
Inspired by the moon, he must also love hide-and-seek,
For I have been searching for those dazzling eyes for long.

Our souls have been intertwined with the same moon's dust.
The moon knows my secrets and how much I trust,
One night when the moon shines its brightest silver beams,
We are going to find each other exactly how I've pictured it in
my dreams.

Maybe you are reading this,
While staring at the luminous moon,
Hoping that our paths cross soon.
I know we are the same, but in different ways, like the moon.

DEAR SEA

Oh, dear sea,
My eyes have yearned for your sight,
My heart has craved to be alright.
Your roaring waves have awakened my inner writer,
By watering my wilted inspiration.

Jealousy is what pricks my hand,
While my feet walk barefoot on your sand.
And suddenly the 'hair-care' girl,
No longer cares about her salty hair with frizz and curl.

I know your romantic ways,
No matter how much you conceal your love from my gaze.
You cool down the sun after a long day of shining hot
and bright,
And the way you kiss the sun goodbye,
Always in the hope to meet again in the morning sky.

The sun loves you too,
It sets every day to immerse in you,
And trusts you not to cheat with the moon,
And rises yet again to provide you warmth after a cold night
of gloom.

THE SEA AND ITS PEACE

Admiring the beauty of the sea,
The peace it holds,
And the serenity it expends.

With the golden hue spreading into the sky,
And merging into the water,
Making the sunlight dance through the crystalline water.

Calmness has surrounded me,
And my mind has stopped thinking all at once.

This is exactly what I needed,
The sea in sight with the crimson sky,
To feel alright.

THE LAKE EXPOSES MY VULNERABILITIES

The crystal-clear lake,
Healing me from all my ache,
Embedded with calm and serenity,
Endows me with a sense of clarity!

The lake reflects my rawness by holding up a mirror,
And down runs my spine a quick shiver,
How beautifully nature has exposed my real self, using the lake's tranquillity,
For the veil was removed and underneath lay my vulnerability!

Seeing the lake with its rippling water,
Made me wonder,
Where I had lost the chirpy little girl in me,
In the pursuit of becoming independent and free.

The rays of sun touching the blue lake,
Ignited a sparkle in my eyes,
To bring the little girl back.
For in the chase of growing up, she was left behind on the track.

Thankful to the lake for reuniting me with myself,
The self which was hazy and lost,
In the journey of life where the stronger me was being raised!

NORTHERN LIGHTS

Astounded I stand,
Witnessing the Northern Lights in the sky from the land.
Seems like the Lights had come to visit us with a surprise,
For not always do the Northern Lights bless the UK skies.

Dancing in the dark sky,
And adding a sparkle in each eye,
Magical and surreal it looks,
Ticking a dream off in everyone's bucket lists and books.

The pink, purple, blue, and green lights,
Add colours to our dull nights,
And life to our dead skies,
Emitting hope and light in the dark before the sun rises.

Family

MY PILLARS OF SUPPORT: MUMMA AND PAPA

Blind trust is what my parents have in me,
They gave me wings to cross the seven seas.

Did everything to see a smile on my face,
So that I come first in life's race.

It takes a lot of courage and a heavy heart to make such a dream come true,
Yet they stood firm and made me as strong as a coffee brew.

Studying abroad was my biggest dream,
It was fulfilled with my family being on my team.

Blessed I am to know such souls like my dad and mom,
Seeing them feels like witnessing the God's biggest blessings in form!

MY WORLD IN THIS BIG WIDE WORLD

You have seen a world without me,
But I have never seen a world without you.
You might not need me, but I will always need you.

I did not witness your childhood the way you embraced mine,
Before me, maybe you were fine,
But before you, I must've waited for the stars to align,
For you are the parents for whom I daily thank the divine.

No need to play 'Win my love' competitions,
For parents have the strength to love beyond conditions.
Everything in this world has a price,
But there's no currency created for parents' sacrifice.

How will I be able to do for you what you have done for me?
For no amount could be close to the love you shower on me.

I've seen you go miles,
Just to see me smile.

You have stood with me against all odds,
Even in times when I was lost in pessimistic thoughts.
So, today, it is me who is confessing,
Being your daughter is no less than a blessing.

YES, BROTHER, I ADORE YOU LIKE A MOTHER

I was in deep sleep when you came,
One more member was added to the family frame.
I woke up, wore my pink frock,
Rushed to the hospital without looking at the clock.

There you were, extremely delicate, with tiny hands and feet,
Your eyes were gigantic and your nose was triangle-shaped.

Immediately felt pride in being the elder one,
For now, I had a brother with whom I'd have lots of fun.
At that moment, I decided to always treasure my little bundle of joy,
Little did I know that one day you would not be so little.

You grew up too fast,
Feels like yesterday when I first held you in my arms,
Your cute little face working on me like a charm.

I may not be the first arms to hold you,
But I promise I will always be there when you need someone to understand you.

Every time you find yourself stuck in a twister,
You know that you can come to your sister.

I will always be there for you, brother,
For I am no less than your mother.

DEAR PAPA

Dear Papa,

To the hands that taught me how to walk,
To the smile on your face when you saw me talk,
To the first man I loved,
To the first person I hugged.
Papa, you were there at all my firsts,
Always protected me from the worsts.

I may not have said it aloud,
But you made everyone very proud.
You worked your way up,
All to provide us milk in a silver cup.

You are my role model, my ideal.
You inspire me in ways which seems unreal.
Yours is an incredible success story,
Which I got to witness with all the glory.

Thank you, Papa, for giving me such a lifestyle,
And for being a person who is so versatile.
Thank you, Papa, for scolding me when needed,
And cheering for me when I succeeded.
All the gratitude in this world is less,
When it's a dad whose love needs no words to be expressed.

MOTHER'S ARMS

Do you know which is the safest place in this world?
A place where the word 'stress' doesn't exist,
A place built on peace, knitted with love, secured with affection, and sewed together with miracles.
Sounds like heaven, right?
Well, this place is a mother's arms.

Feels like heaven is proud and honoured,
To be compared to a mother's arms.

A mother's arm is like a shield,
It has the power to protect and heal.

Being away from my mother makes me crave the warmth of her arms,
For her prayers have always protected me from every harm.

It has been a long time since I had a peaceful nap,
I can't wait to go back and sleep like a baby in her lap.

For the first time, I am feeling short of words,
For even the uncountable words in a dictionary cannot describe the feeling of being in my mother's arms.

EVERY MOM'S DESIRE

For once, she wants to stop being strong,
And see if the world is strong enough to accept her if she falls.

For once, she wants to stop taking care,
And start being taken care of.

For once, she wants to stop thinking about everyone,
And start being thought about.

For once, she wants to stop celebrating all,
And start being celebrated.

For once, she wants to stop nurturing the family dynamics,
And start being nurtured.

For once, she wants to stop watering the plants,
And start to water her inner soul.

For once, she wants to stop hugging and kissing her kids,
And start being hugged and kissed by her kids.

For once, she wants to stop juggling between work and home,
And start and end her day however she likes.

For once, she wants to stop being a role model,
And become who she was before she became a mom.

—Just for once, let her be the one she was before she became a mom.

DEAR GRANDMA

Dear Maa (Grandma),

I remember the way you braided my hair,
Got me ready for school with so much love and care.

The way you feed me from your hand whenever I am upset,
I know you might forget your medicine but you will
never forget,
To check if I had my meals on time or not.

The way you act as my lawyer,
Every time someone says or does something against me,
And the way you are always fighting for me (sometimes even
with your own son).

I will always love you and cherish your motherly love towards
me.
You may not have given birth to me,
But you will always be my mother,
For you will always be my loving 'Maa'.

—Love you, Maa

TO PAVITRA, MY FAMILY AWAY FROM HOME

Sometimes I think, what if it wasn't raining that day?
What if I wasn't stuck inside the learning grid?
What if I had an umbrella to escape?
Would our paths still cross the way it did?

The universe works magically to merge the paths of two people.
Seeing how I struggled to find genuine people and friends,
The universe instructed the rains from the clouds to descend.

Heavy rains and no umbrellas left us helpless,
That day, Rajasthan met Gujarat on English land,
Too naive to understand the purpose of us shaking hands,
Little did we know that we would end up becoming each
other's biggest help at university.

I now know that I couldn't have done university
without you,
Because you were the one among many and few,
Who not only laughed but cried with me too.
I can never forget the endless laughter we've shared,
And all the meals that we prepared.

We liked the same people and hated the same enemies,
We were together in every memory.
Thank you for making my experience worthwhile,
Because of you, I could survive those days with a smile!

Life Lessons

THE ART OF LISTENING

The world has given them enough suggestions,
To be confused between the answers to all their questions.
Everyone has judged them without listening to their story,
Going through a rough patch with days and nights being stormy.

Provide them a listening ear,
When they come to you to share their fear.
Maybe they want no opinion or advice,
But just a pair of patient ears to hear them out sometimes.

Be all ears and no words,
For they need an open mind and accepting heart to be heard.
Maybe God has chosen you as their lifeboat,
To save them from drowning and to bring them afloat.

This small act of lending an ear to those in need,
Can change their lives' direction and speed.
Quietly listening and wiping away their tears,
And assuring that you are there for them with all your prayers.

And if possible, also hear what they don't say out loud,
For you don't know the intensity of the pain they've endured.
Just hug them tight and give them a ray of hope that is new,
and say, "I am always there for you."

PERFECTIONISM: A MYTH

Perfectionism will rob you of your peace,
In its chase, your happiness will begin to cease.
Why do you want to be perfect,
When you can be as free as a bird by being imperfect?

Perfectionism being a myth and unattainable,
Will impede your success in ways that are unbelievable.
Everyone has strengths and weaknesses,
The Almighty created us to preserve our uniqueness.

Perfectionism will always make you question yourself,
Make you envious of someone else.
Accepting the imperfections of humankind,
Is the key to a healthy soul, body, and mind.

Perfectionism will never let you take the first step,
It'll make you doubt your prep.
You will never be hundred percent ready and be perfect
to do it,
But you have to take a leap of faith and trust your inner voice
That says, "You can do it!"

WHAT WILL PEOPLE SAY?

"What will people say?"
A thought with which we struggle every day.
These four words hold the power to reverse your decisions,
Making you question your dreams and visions.

Stop allowing people from entering your mind,
And playing vicious games from behind.
Protect your inner self from outside energy,
Don't let them interfere with your synergy.

You can't stop some people from talking behind your back,
For they are frustrated souls who have lost their track.
Their opinions about you are not worth giving a thought,
What you think about yourself transforms you from weak
to strong.

Limit yourself from discussing dreams, plans, and goals
With those who fail to understand the magnificence of
your soul.
God has given you the power to envision your dream and aim,
So, just believe in your strength to win this game.

GLITTER AND GOLD

Not everyone who talks to you in a friendly manner is a friend,
Some people are disguised as friends and all they do is pretend.
Beware of those people who try to mess up your vibrations,
Because they are capable of destroying your foundations.

Is it quantity or quality that matters in a kinship?
Quantity will always make you restless and unfulfilled in all your friendships,
As the saying goes, "Excess of anything is bad",
It is applicable to friendships too.
However, quality will give you solace and satisfaction to a great extent.

Not all friendships last a lifetime,
Some merely exist to teach you a lesson,
They come, spend time with you and leave you for your own protection.
So, don't sob over broken bonds, instead be grateful for the realisation.

But oh, that rare bond which is curated by the universe,
Which has the ability to turn into blessing every curse,
Such a phenomenon is like gold dust—rare and invaluable.
Just like sugar and water which are soluble,
That bond will also be inseparable.

DRIVEN BY PASSION

Young minds yearning for a degree with first class rank,
All in hopes to get good figures in bank.

Being caught in the rat race,
They've forgotten to reflect true emotions on their face.

"I want to be different," says a little voice at the back of my mind.
My heart echoes, "Be prepared to struggle to have your autograph signed,
And then see how the stars get aligned."

It takes persistence and full faith in the universe,
To have satisfaction, happiness, and money in your purse.

Let me follow my passion,
And show the world how to fulfil dreams in my fashion.

No one is my competition,
For my goals and plans are different from other people's ambition.

Let's all support the aspirations of our peers,
So that in the end, we can all be happy with no tears.

TRAVELLING: A WAY TO RE-DEFINE YOURSELF

Travelling will change you.
You will never be the same again
Once you step out and choose not to remain
Stagnant in the same place.

Travelling will enrich your thoughts,
And suddenly the unknown will cease to haunt.
For once you step out of your home,
Your heart will always crave to roam
New places, no matter how many times you return home.

Travelling will heighten your intellect,
And as your bucket list gets checked,
The urge to embark on novel experiences will amplify,
And exploring the world will become your new high.

Travelling will change your perspective about the world,
Each time you return home after exploring a new place,
You will perceive everything with a different pair of eyes,
Eyes which have seen the sunrise and sunset from a different corner of the Earth!

MAYBE WRONG HAPPENS FOR RIGHT TO HAPPEN

Maybe you have to feel sorrow and cry,
To appreciate the happiness that will come by.

Maybe you have to be heartbroken,
To cherish love with pure emotions.

Maybe you have to go through phases of being alone,
To not take granted the feeling of 'home.'

Maybe you have to feel someone's absence,
To admire their presence.

Maybe some things need to end,
To save you from a foe disguised as a friend.

Maybe you have to taste cruelty,
To show the world how kindness is the real beauty.

Maybe you have to endure darkness in the noon,
To shine at night like the moon.

So, for now, keep going without questioning why,
Because sometimes somethings have to go wrong,
For the right things to come along.

MIND VERSUS HEART

The only battle worth losing,
Which ends in your heart and mind bruising,
Is the one that you fight with yourself every day.

Winning is impossible when the heart is at odds with the mind,
The outcome being to lose yourself and never being able to find.

Mind accepts the truth faster and way before,
Which the heart tries to avoid and ignore.
Mind is the mature adult living inside you,
But your heart is still the little kid always demanding something new.

Don't let the adult overpower your inner child,
And stop lying to yourself in the name of pride.
Lying will provide temporary comfort,
And a baggage full of grief and hurt.

Stop being your own victim and culprit,
Instruct your heart and mind to just quit!
Quit playing the vicious game of perplexity,
And live together in harmony without any complexity.

Let the heart be the heart and mind be the mind,
Let the heart be emotional and mind practical.
Don't force a change that is unadaptable.
Remember, it's the heart that feels and the mind that thinks,
And this fusion together brings all the wins.

STANDSTILL AND STUCK

Life took a pause,
And a traffic jam became the cause.
Going back was not a possibility,
And driving forward seemed to be a matter of impossibility.

All the vehicles lined up unable to move,
Blaring horns for the traffic to improve.
Drivers became restless and frustrated,
And criticised the traffic rules curated by the educated.

The traffic won't clear,
No matter how much you panic, complain, or shed a tear.
The traffic will move when it has to,
So why not just sit back, relax, and appreciate the view?

The choice is yours to remain calm or to lose control,
So, appreciate the stillness and relax your soul.
Enjoy the pause because life moves fast,
In the blink of an eye, this traffic jam will become a matter of the past.

DEAR HARD WORKER

Dear hard worker,

Take a break,
Not for the world but for your sake,
For you deserve to restore your sanity,
And bring your lost soul back to gravity.

Self-reflect, cleanse, and de-clutter your busy mind,
Take a step back from the daily grind,
Listen to the voiceless echoes in your head,
And speak to yourself the words which otherwise
remain unsaid.

And when you finally decide to pause,
Do not feel guilty for missing the calls.
You are worthy of your rest,
For you have worked hard and given your best.

TRUE HAPPINESS

In a world where people wear masks,
Finding true happiness can be a task.

What happiness means to you,
Might mean to me something new.

One's happiness should come from within,
It should not depend on another's rhythm.

Staying happy gives you a glow,
Makes the heart as pure as snow,
And makes you progress fast and not slow.

Happiness provides a strange tranquillity to one's existence,
Gives the power to achieve one's desires with persistence.

A smiling face is always appealing,
But I'll tell you, a smiling heart is a completely different feeling!

HEART OF GOLD

Is it a blessing or a curse to be a good person?
For the world is cruel for certain.

Why do people only care to receive?
Why do people deceive?
Why do people bear so much hate against other souls?
Why do people criticise the ones who fail to achieve their goals?

Why can't we become better human beings?
For once let us all take a break,
And think about giving for the world's sake.
Let's pour out kindness and humanity wherever we go,
And shower compassion and selflessness to help
people grow.

To all the good-hearted people out there,
I know at times it becomes difficult to care,
I know the world has failed you many times,
And I also know how easy it is for people to cross their lines.

But hold on to your generous attitude,
Do not let the world's perception turn you rude.
Do not ever regret having a soft heart,
Because people like you are like fine art.

Specially curated and crafted by God,
The God who made everyone an even but warm-hearted people an odd,
Odd because we can't be divided but can surely multiply.

The world might have failed you,
But don't ever let yourself fail the world,
For you are the hope and faith,
On which the world is surviving with so much weight.

DEAR OVERTHINKER

Dear Overthinker,

I feel you when thoughts flood your mind,
And how a random thought becomes difficult to fight.
I feel you when everything affects so deeply,
And absorbs into the heart so completely.

I too have spent sleepless nights,
Worrying about things that might not even see the daylight.

It's fascinating how our mood changes,
From being happy to emotional all at a variety of ranges.

Overthinking seems like a blessing wrapped in a curse,
Curse when we lose ourselves in search of unanswered questions,
And blessing when nothing in this world is uncertain to us,
For we have already thought about everything—from a pin
to an airplane.

FLOWERS BLOOM INSIDE YOUR HEART

Our biggest mistake is searching for miracles outside,
And being a stranger to the power we hold inside.
Something as powerful and sacred as a miracle can never appear in the exterior,
It can only be created and felt in the interior.

You will be surprised, when you take a peek within yourself,
To witness a volcano of miracles waiting to erupt;
Waiting because your heart is corrupt,
Corrupt for holding grudges and insensitive thoughts.

Once you let go of unnecessary thoughts,
And untie all the heavy knots,
You have unknowingly or knowingly found the cure,
The cure which will make your heart pure.

Be ready to witness all the wonders of life,
For you are now healed from all the impurities.
Now is the time to give yourself a chance and a belief,
And, let the magic happen with a relief.

YOU CAN'T WIN AGAINST TIME

I was panicking about my future,
Thinking of doing everything sooner,
Worried that time was running out,
And disturbed by negative thoughts.

The comforting words from my father calmed me down,
He said, "You can't win against time,
So stop trying to fight against it,
Everything will happen at its own pace,
No need to rush because it isn't a race."

Worrying about the future won't do you any good,
For nothing can prevent the inevitable,
However, time will never stop you from creating your pace.

Sometimes things are not in our hands,
So it's best to allow time to take the command,
For time is the greatest healer,
As it always passes away and stops for no leader.

Bad times will make you strong,
To appreciate the good times that come along.
Maybe we are in a hurry,
But time says, "My child, don't worry,
For we have plenty of time."

THE ALCHEMY OF IMAGINATION

Your imagination is a portal to reality,
With no limits and spreading up to eternity,
You got to live your dream in your head,
To turn it into reality before you are dead.

What you speak, visualise, and think,
Holds the power to manifest in a blink,
So, be careful with every word and thought,
For one negative belief or phrase might come at a great cost.

Leave no room for doubts or hesitations,
Do not compromise your dreams in any situation,
Never restrict your imagination,
For you are worthy of living all your dreams.

THE ANSWERS RESIDE WITHIN YOU

The answers you are looking for outside,
Reside within you, and all it requires is the right sight,
To have a peek inside,
And find out your inner guide.

You will be your greatest guide,
Your intuition will provide
What the outer world could not,
For you are everything you'll ever need to untangle the knot.

Rely completely on your sixth sense,
For it will act in your defence,
It won't let anything wrong befall you,
Just trust it to lead you through.

Trust yourself when trusting the world seems difficult,
For the world is made of greed with little scope of being humbled,
And so, turn your head inside,
And there you will find all the right answers that you were
desperately looking for in the wrong places.

YOU ARE COMPLETE, ENTIRE, AND WHOLE

You are not just a book,
That is read once and kept aside.
You are a whole library!

You are not just a flower,
That is plucked for being too pretty.
You are a beautiful garden adorned with hundreds of flowers!

You are not just stars in the sky,
Dimmed by the moon's radiance.
You are an entire galaxy carrying all the stars and the moon!

You are not just a wave,
Rising and falling with the wind,
You are an ocean whose depth cannot be fathomed!

You are not just a rock,
Waiting to be moulded and used.
You are an entire mountain standing tall and touching the clouds!

You are not a missing piece,
Trying to fit in.
You are an entire puzzle—complete and whole!

—You are not a part of a whole, you are an entire whole.

EMBRACE YOUR TRUE SELF

Stop hiding your true self,
Stop pretending to be someone else.
Accept your rawness,
Because no one is flawless.

Don't push away your anxieties, frustrations, and fears,
It is okay to let them out in tears,
Feel them so completely,
That you never feel them again so deeply.

When your soul is full of doubts,
How can you expect to have contentment found?
By letting the misery out, you will grab the power to harness,
And make space for happiness, joy, and calmness.

Don't let your fears rob you of your joys.
Remember, you own your emotions,
Your emotions don't own you,
So don't let them control you.

A FEW LEARNINGS

Learn to be present for yourself,
The world can wait until you become what you're
meant to be.
Don't let the world happen to you,
For you are meant to happen to the world.

Learn to respect your inner self,
For your mind has become a battlefield,
Battling all the negativities every day,
And facing all the challenges with a smile day by day.

Learn to love yourself,
For love has to be soaked inside,
Before giving it to others outside,
Otherwise, love ends up becoming mere infatuation.

Learn to be patient when things don't go your way,
Let the unpredictable happen,
Stop, breathe, and take no action,
The future might be better than your prediction.

Learn to forgive yourself for the sins committed in the past,
Because the future ahead is vast.
Your present is not worth sacrificing for a past that will never return,
And your present is too short to worry about a future that might never come.

Learn to stop being a people-pleaser,
And not entertain disrespect from any creature.
Maintain distance from people who suck up your energy,
For these people are your enemies, disguised as friendly.

Most importantly, learn to celebrate your life,
Not only on birthdays, but every day.
Celebrate your success but don't forget the failures,
That provide the steps towards a brighter and successful life.

YOURSELF

You have to be recognised by yourself,
For the world to recognise you.
You have to believe in yourself,
For the world to believe in you.
You have to be proud of yourself,
For the world to be proud of you.
You have to listen to yourself,
For the world to listen to you.
You have to speak to yourself,
For the world to speak to you.
You have to love yourself,
For the world to love you.
You have to be kind to yourself,
For the world to be kind to you.
You have to be your own priority,
For the world to treat you as a priority.
You have to accept yourself with all your flaws,
For the world to accept you as you are—raw and authentic.

It isn't selfish to put yourself first,
Because you will always be with yourself during the worst!
So, it's you that you have to hold on to,
And the world around and everything else will fall in
place too!

FEEL IT TILL YOU HEAL FROM IT

The girl weeping on a bench in a park,
Seeking comfort and light from a stranger (me) when everything around her was dark.
Giving her a handkerchief to wipe away her tears,
I told her that I was all ears.

She spoke about how full of life she was before he happened,
How he drained the life out of her and left her broken and miserable,
How she could not remember who she was before the pain embodied her,
Because she had become used to feeling this way for a long time now.

Listening to her, I gave her a warm hug,
And a hope of "You'll come out stronger from this."

Little did I know that all she really wanted was to cry her heart out,
It was okay if she did not want to be strong,
Did not want to cover herself with a curtain of pretence,
And fool her mind that everything was alright when nothing truly was.

She was venting all her feelings out in the form of tears,
To feel every little emotion so intensely so that she eventually heals from it.

I hope and pray that she has healed herself from the trauma,
For I was able to relate to her,
Because just like she used tears to let her emotions out,
I use words and poems to let my feelings out.

YOU ARE GOD'S CHILD

You are God's child,
He will never leave your hand in the wild,
And unlike other people around,
He will never forsake and abandon you alone on the ground.

You are God's child,
You will always find him by your side,
He will never take your love and faith for granted,
For he is the one who got the prayers in your heart planted!

You are God's child,
He will always walk in front of you and not behind,
He will pave the path and prepare the roads,
So that you can walk fearlessly without being slowed.

You are God's child,
He has seen the way you smiled,
And has also heard your prayers and silent cries,
He knows even when you don't tell him everyone's lies,
He has seen and heard what you did not,
He is your sole witness,
So, be patient and wait for his justice.

You are God's child,
Let go of the doubts and fears that you carry in your mind,
Trust him completely that he can turn your dreams into
a reality.
Forget the 'how' and focus on your inner spirituality,
For God will never let you down,
So, believe him and take a deep dive for your dreams,
For he will keep you afloat and never let you drown!

VOICE OF THE UNIVERSE

It's the universe's love language
Sings, intuitions and gut feelings which are not average.
The universe is always trying to speak and guide,
If only you hear and put your fears aside.

Against the will of the universe you go,
When you ignore your instincts and tread where your fears flow.
You feel a certain way for a reason,
You must go with your sixth sense in every season.

You are a child of the universe,
An entire galaxy is entangled in your blood and nerves.
You are bestowed with the power
To manifest and achieve your purpose at the right hour.

The universe is ready to grant,
But only if you are ready to plant
The seeds of blind trust, because
A stubborn heart is what the universe loves.

But I must warn you
To not confuse the universe each time you see something new.
Be precise and clear, but not limited,
Pray for your desires but don't get pivoted.

THE ART OF SELFLESSNESS

How do you always end up giving more?
And never find yourself lacking in love and kindness to pour?
Even when sometimes you receive way less than what
you give,
You still choose to radiate to the world everything positive!

Maybe you give not with the intention to receive back,
And that's why there is no amount of hatred that could attack
Your inner peace and crumble your selfless intentions,
For you believe in good deeds with no mentions.

How naive you are to think that everyone has a heart
like yours,
For not everyone endures
With a smile on their face every hateful remark,
And that's why people like you will never have anyone dim
your spark!

At times, overwhelmed you might feel,
For you too crave something that you give with unconditional
zeal.
But don't let the emotionless world stop you from giving,
Keep radiating hope, kindness, and help people winning.

Remember, you are blessed to be a giver,
And what you are looking for outside is already flowing inside you like a river.
You have within you that which everyone seeks elsewhere,
And this is your strength which makes you rare.

LOST IS THE NEW FOUND

The charm of getting lost on unknown roads,
With no maps to follow, just the path as it decodes,
Without thinking of a destination,
For you know that the roads will guide you towards
your location.

Not everything can be planned with precision,
Sometimes there's no option but to make a
spontaneous decision,
And this might deviate you from the original route,
For paths need to be changed and turns must be taken to achieve
your pursuits.

The paths ahead might be hazy to your eyes,
For you have just started your journey towards the rise.
Stop being myopic in your visions,
And start trusting your decisions.

Sometimes being lost is the only way to be found,
So, take a deep breath and look around,
You might meet a version of yourself which is new,
The you who will always walk fearlessly and lead you through!

IT'S ALL GOING TO BE OKAY

It's all going to be okay,
And this feeling of everything falling apart will go away,
Life will be beautiful again,
For there is always sunshine after the rain.

It's all going to be okay,
You will heal and things will mend,
For the sufferings are not permanent,
And just like that, the pain will end.

It's all going to be okay,
You will be happy once more,
In fact, more than before,
So, until then, smile through the scars that you once wore.

It's all going to be okay,
The worry and fear are not here to stay,
Maybe they are here to go away after making you pay,
For the sins you may have committed in some past life,
To make your soul liberated from all its debts.

It's all going to be okay.
Who are you to think it's not going to be okay?
Surrender it to time, the healer,
And once again your eyes will shine like a dreamer.

SURRENDER IT TO GOD

Surrender it to God
When things don't go your way,
For if it is not going your way then it is happening as per
God's say.

Surrender it to God
When a situation starts slipping out of your hands,
Allow God to take complete control and follow
his commands.

Surrender it to God
When nothing around you makes sense,
For God is the only one who can bring clarity by removing
the suspense.

Surrender it to God
When you don't get what you desire,
Maybe God wants you to achieve even higher.

Surrender it to God
When you are filled with anxiety and doubt,
For he is the only one who can make the seeds sprout.

Surrender it to God
When the path ahead is unclear,
For he is your life's steer.

Surrender it to God,
Everything connected to you—including your entire being,
And watch how God takes care of your well-being.

THE WORLD CAN BE SELFISH

While you were helping them fly,
They were busy clipping your wings.

While you were supporting them to rise above,
They were busy conspiring for you to sink below.

While you were showering their heart with warmth and love,
They were busy hollowing you out.

While you were bringing light to their darkness,
They were busy pushing you towards gloom.

While you were healing and uniting them together,
They were busy breaking you apart.

While you were opening new doors for them,
They were busy closing all doors for you.

—Be selective about whose dimmed light you choose to brighten.

IT'S YOU

You are the writer of your story,
You have the power to turn your adversities into your glory.
You are the protagonist,
For you don't revolve around the plot, the plot revolves around you.

You are the poet of your poetry,
You have the strength to instil rhythm, theme, tone, or all three
Into your life and make it rhyme,
For loving and moulding your life is not a crime.

You are the painter of your canvas,
Take control of the brush,
Choose the prettiest colours,
And paint a life worth a recall.

You are the designer of your life,
Pick up the scissors and cut out the parts you despise.
Stitch together the broken fragments,
For you deserve to reach heights and not remain stagnant.

You are the curator of your legacy,
Embrace your journey's ups and downs with ecstasy.
You are not the history that is forgotten,
You are a future legacy worth a million celebrations!

'NEW YOU'

There is absolutely nothing wrong with feeling broken
and empty.
It means a space has been created within you for God to enter and take command of your life by awakening your soul while guiding you towards the light.
God is creating a 'new you' where feeling empty is just a process of this enlightened creation.
This 'new you' will not be afraid and will be capable of conquering all your deepest desires.
So, for now, embrace the emptiness because it is only this way for a while, and trust the tables to turn. Soon, everything will be onwards and upwards.

—It is only this way for a while.

STOP HAVING A BACK-UP PLAN

When you have a backup plan ready, it will never allow you to use your full potential. It will always keep pulling you backwards instead of pushing you forward towards the original plan.

Having a plan B would force you to give up and take a step back from the original plan at every minor inconvenience. Do not make the mistake of falling prey to this trap and never ditch your plan A to settle for plan B.

—Stop playing safe. Take risks. Never settle for anything less. Go after what you truly desire.

DESTINATION VERSUS JOURNEY

As appealing as the destination may seem to be,
It's the journey, with its ups and downs, that is worth it truly.
So, do not forget to live through your journey,
For once the destination arrives (which will arrive eventually),
there won't be much to live for!

∞

Love

LOVE MY LIFE WITH THE LOVE OF MY LIFE

What do I desire?
Or should I say, "What does being happy require?"
A life story from which I never want to retire,
Or a love story which never loses its fire?

Love story is the river which eventually,
Blends with the sea like life story.
Make the latter a priority,
And see how the former blooms with prosperity.

I don't want to wait for the love of my life,
To start loving my life.
Life will always be celebrated and loved,
And even more with the love of my life.

—The love of my life will come sooner or later, but my life will not come again.

THREE TYPES OF LOVE

Worth dying for: love for your parents

Worth killing for: love for your kids

Worth living for: love for your life partner

ALL ABOUT LOVE

Aren't tears the purest form of love?
For no pair of eyes can be enough,
Without the tears of happiness and joy,
Which comes with being in a love story!

Aren't prayers a way of expressing love?
For no two lovers can be together without the blessing
from above!
The prayers cross the barriers of distance and time,
To reach the one who is just mine!

Aren't dreams a way to meet your other half?
When the universe decides to put the two on opposite sides of
a graph,
Closing eyes becomes the easiest route,
To feel their presence without any dispute.

Aren't unexpected calls the best way to care?
For they are the ones with whom you share
All your chaos and excitement without any pretence,
And the only call that you never want to end!

LOVE WILL FIND YOU

What makes you think you won't find love again?
Is it the heartbreak that created an empty void within?
Or is it because the line between trust and blind trust is too thin?
Whatever it is, if you won't find love then love will come and find you!

Even when you give up on love,
Love won't give up on you,
No matter how much you try to hide,
Or surround yourself with darkness,
Love will find you, and towards the light it will guide.

No, you are not difficult to love,
Someone out there is praying for a love like yours,
And is fluent in reciprocating exactly the kind of love
That you've craved your entire life.
And one day you both will find each other,
And this time, the search will end,
For it will be God-sent!

TRUE LOVE

True love won't knock on your door,
It will just barge in without the need for you to explore,
For one does not knock at one's home,
One just steps in as if it was their own!

Yes, true love arrives without any prior caution,
And no, it doesn't make your heart flutter and winds storm.
But yes, it brings in peace, comfort, and solace to your heavy heart,
And a big yes, that true love would be the easiest journey to start!

Your true love is exclusively meant for you,
No other being can snatch it from you,
For your true love is intertwined with your soul,
And it comes to you at the perfect time without you having to control.

DEAR SOULMATE

Dear soulmate/life partner/love of my life,

Have we met yet?
Or are we yet to meet?

Maybe I have not yet had a chance to feel your presence,
But how deeply I feel your absence.

See you at the right time (hopefully soon)!

LOVE IS YOU AND YOU ARE LOVE

Stop seeking outside what you already have inside.
Love is what you already have within yourself,
And one does not search for what one already has.

Remember,
Love and you are not separate,
Love is you and you are love,
You are curated from love, by love, to love, and to be loved!

Love is deeply rooted in your heart,
You can never run out of it,
No matter how much you expend it on the wrong people.
Maybe they needed your love to learn about love,
So never regret giving love,
For the world needs more of it.

Before giving up on love,
Remember the way you love,
And this is all the hope you'll ever need
To find someone who can reciprocate the intense yet calm love that you intend to radiate.

RISING IN LOVE

There is no such thing as 'falling in love',
For if you can fall in, you might fall out as well.

One does not jump into dark oceans without a life jacket,
But there is no limit to soaring high above and touching
the sky.
So, it is never about falling but always about 'rising in love'.

STOP THE ANSWERS, AND ASK ME THE QUESTIONS

Answers, answers everywhere,
Google has the answers to all questions out there.
This world has every answer,
From the lyrics of a song to the steps of a dancer.

Overwhelmed by the number of answers and suggestions,
Now I just want to be asked these simple questions—
"Did you eat food? What can I do to improve your mood?
Are you doing okay? How was your day?"

The answers to these questions might not reach the world's ears,
For these simple questions are rarely asked by any peers.
We can't simplify a world so complicated
By just answers, only to forget the simple questions to be stated.

The answers to these questions are beautiful and full of feelings,
But only if someone cares enough to ask these questions with meaning,
Someone who wants to hear, not to react but to respond,
If you have that 'someone', never break that bond.

STOP SETTLING

Stop settling for lukewarm coffee when you can have steaming hot coffee providing you comfort on cold days or an iced latte quenching your thirst on a warm sunny day.

—*This is not about coffee!*

SOMEONE OUT THERE IS WAITING FOR YOU

When everything stops making sense,
And you find yourself trapped in chaos and a mess,
Find peace in this thought that,
There's a person waiting for you,
Once you have been through all the phases you were meant to complete and go through alone, in this journey called 'life'.
This person will be waiting at the other end to love and be loved by you.
Be patient till the universe decides to merge your path with your person,
And when that happens, in that heavenly moment,
All your questions and prayers will be answered.

IT'S ALWAYS ABOUT WHO STAYED

It is never about who left and came back,
It is always about who came and never left,
Even when everyone was against you and roads ahead were blurry,
Standing at the crossroads, they walked on the path that led them towards you.

It is never about who left you midway,
It is always about who held your hand and never walked away.
As harsh as it may sound, it can't be love if it is not fought,
And stood for against all odds.

It is never about who was there in your good times,
It is always about who wiped your tears in your challenging times.
For people may come and go,
But it is always about the ones who stay despite the highs and lows.

YOUR SOULMATE WILL FIND YOU

For once, stop searching for your soulmate,
And let your soulmate search for you.

—Maybe this time, your soulmate will find you.

Wistful Musings

A PLANE FLYING IN THE WIDE SKY

Sitting in the park with a novel in my hands,
Feeling the wind ruffling my hair strands,
Everything seemed so serene and calm,
With the waterfall flowing and flowers blooming in their own charm.

Amidst this serenity, a whirring sound came from the sky,
I lifted my head up and looked through the clouds, wide-eyed,
Saw a plane flying against the wind and between the clouds.

It seemed like a tiny plane at such a great height,
People on the land cannot fathom a flying plane's might.
To see its grandness, one has to reach a certain altitude,
And always climb up in life with gratitude.

How strong that plane must be,
For it is carrying numerous emotions at the same time—
Emotions of leaving one's family,
Feelings of returning home happily,
Or excitement of a vacation with family.

A small wish passed through my mind,
To be on that plane which was flying against the wind,
And look out of the window,
And be excited for the next destination to arrive.

CHANDRAYAN 3

The moon seemed far away,
Until today, when India achieved what it prayed for.
The tricolour was rooted on the silver land after much toil,
Leaving behind a legacy to be celebrated on Indian soil.

Looking at the moon tonight,
With pride and respect for India to reach such a height.
It was definitely a difficult climb,
For it had to fail twice to be successful the third time.

What India did today will be written in golden words,
And the noise of success will be loud enough to be heard all over the world.
First country to land on the south pole of the moon,
It is just the beginning for India to turn dreams into reality soon.

The satellite carried every Indian's wish, prayer, and emotion,
And delivered them to the moon with utmost devotion.
Hat's off to the Indian Space Research Organisation,
I am proud to be a citizen of such a great nation.

SILENT DESTROYERS: DRINKING AND SMOKING

What has happened to this generation?
Where drinking and smoking has overshadowed the real you,
The you, who is hidden behind drunk nights,
The you, who is trying to forget more than remember,
And the you, who is constantly muffling away your emotions and temper.

Why find pleasure in drinking and smoking,
When you know in the end it is you who is choking?

In a world where you can drink anything,
Why drink the bitter alcohol,
When it has the capacity to take away your everything?

It takes courage to be different, to be the odd one out,
Not as easy as being among the crowd.
Standing alone is scary but powerful,
And a life without alcohol and cigarettes is surely wonderful!

Feel proud to not be a smoker and drinker,
As I don't need alcohol or cigarettes to be a thinker!

BEAUTY CAN'T BE SEEN, IT CAN ONLY BE EXPERIENCED

Do we have to look a certain way,
To fit into the word 'beautiful', like people say?
Does being beautiful require a perfect figure, extra fair skin,
Long, shiny hair and not short-till-chin?

I feel your extra fair complexion can't make you pretty,
Solely based on your outer beauty.
Your white face is of no use,
When you judge people of colour with your insensitive views.

I know some people who are obsessed with fair skin,
Discriminating against coloured skin and unknowingly committing a sin.
It takes more than just a pair of eyes to appreciate your beauty,
Because beauty is not limited to what eyes can see, but also what hearts can feel.

Being a wheatish-coloured girl,
I've been compared to the skin which is as white as a pearl.
I've grown to be comfortable and happy in my own colour and skin,
Despite some people playing the colour card to prick me like a pin.

Beauty is not in a person but in the perspective,
Some visualise Lord Ganesh in an elephant,
But some can only envision a piece of rock in Lord Ganesh.
It's the way you see and feel which makes the difference.

UNSEEN WOUNDS

She is a victim
In this patriarchal system.
She feels uncomfortable and unsafe,
When she deals with the dirty male gaze.

She is no object
For your inappropriate touch to collect.
Her dressing up and looking beautiful
Doesn't give men the right to think that she is useable.

She, who clearly says no,
Is still misunderstood by the boys who refuse to grow.
She has no age limit,
Some men treat even a six-month-old or a sixty-year-old as an exhibit.

He, who thinks a 'no' can hurt his ego and esteem,
He, who can't hear a woman's silent cry and scream,
Is a beast in the body of a human.
For a true man understands a 'no' without any confusion.

Every time she steps outside alone,
She turns on the live location on her phone,
Praying not to be a part of yet another harassment that the newspaper prints daily,
And to reach her destination safely.

When will the world understand,
And make her feel safe and calm her trembling hand?
She is more than just her body,
She is a human with a heart like nobody.

FORGIVING THEM

With agony in her heart,
Tears in her eyes,
And pain in her trembling voice,
Forgiving them was her only choice.

It took all her strength to gather herself,
And pull herself out of the grief,
And despite the ache that pushed her to the edge,
Her heart decided upon forgiveness over revenge!

With forgiveness, her suffering collapsed,
The chains that caged her broke open,
With a rush of relief spreading through her body,
For she had let go of the bonds which were already broken!

She was not tied to her past anymore,
And finally, she chose to restore,
And bring back her peace that people stole,
And now it was she who was in control.

UNFALLEN TEARS, UNEXPRESSED FEELINGS, AND UNVOICED WORDS

The tears almost at the brim,
Clouding the eyes and the surroundings becoming dim,
Just one stroke of strength,
And forced are the tears to flow back in.

The feelings just about to outburst,
And rupture the endless emotions immersed,
Just one instance of hesitation,
And the feelings once again fail in their communication.

The words on the verge of being voiced,
To clear up the head's noise,
Pause at the lips by the fear of being judged,
And decide to roll back the tongue and remain caged.

The unfallen tears, unexpressed feelings, and the unvoiced words,
Are fatigued from being the heart's silent screams,
And tired of being concealed.
They are bearing the punishment of being locked up for
backing out just before the finish line!

DRAWING STARS AROUND HER SCARS

How gracefully she adorns each one of her scar,
Given to her by people who were once near and now far.

The world is unaware,
Of how the hurt left her in despair.
For she never chose to share,
Her side of the story to the world
But just to God in her prayer!

Holding onto the last rays of hope all this while,
She hid her pain behind that smile.
Knowing that she is broken inside,
Look how put together she still looked outside.

Each scar she owns has a story,
Which, with courage, she turned into her glory.
The scars symbolise the battles she has gone through,
And survived the pain which only she knew.

Using her pain as fuel for her desire,
And not allowing it to backfire,
She turned her plight upside down,
And celebrated her survival through the battles,
That now reside on her head like a crown.

ACKNOWLEDGEMENT

To Lord Hanuman, thank you for always being with me, blessing me and guiding me towards my highest purpose.

To Mumma and Papa, thank you for believing in me and my dreams.

To Yuvraj, thank you for always being my support system.

To all my Family, I love you all to the moon and back.

To Sania, Jahanvi, Shobhita and Pavitra, thank you for being my best friends and soul sisters.

And finally, to the universe, thank you for all the magic in my life.

ABOUT THE AUTHOR

Karishma Kothari went to the UK to pursue her graduation in Economics three years ago. Surprisingly, the country not only provided her with the best education but also woke up the inner poet within which she never knew she had. This new inspiration helped her to turn feelings into words and emotions into poems.

Karishma writes what she feels so that her readers can also feel what they read. Through her poems, she wants to string the right chords in the reader's hearts and have them experience the depths of emotions that she has inculcated in each of her poems.

Her poems revolve around nature, overthinking, loneliness, moving abroad, her own feelings, friendships, heartbreaks, love, family, and many more such heartfelt and deep topics. This poetry book will allow the readers to relate themselves to the poems they read and delve into a world of poetry that Karishma has created.